THE

INSANITY

OF

EMPIRE:

A Book of Poems
Against the Iraq War

By Robert Bly

Published by Ally Press, 524 Orleans St., St. Paul, MN 55107

Printed in the United States of America

Design by Susan Lee

Bly, Robert
The Insanity of Empire /Robert Bly. — 1st Edition, April 2004.

0-915408-57-0

Ally Press
524 Orleans St.
St. Paul, MN 55107

www.catalog.com/ally
pferoe@comcast.net

OTHER BOOKS BY ROBERT BLY OF RELATED INTEREST

A Poetry Reading Against the Vietnam War, editor, with
David Ray, Sixties Press, 1966

Forty Poems Touching on Recent American History, editor,
Beacon Press, 1970

The Teeth Mother Naked at Last, City Lights, 1970

Sleeping Joining Hands, Harper and Row, 1973

Meditations on the Insatiable Soul, HarperCollins, 1994

CONTENTS

I

Call and Answer

Advice from the Geese

Let Sympathy Pass

The Stew of Discontents

II

The Executive's Death

Watching Television

Come With Me

Those Being Eaten

A Glimpse of American History

Sleet Storm on the Merritt Parkway

III

The Alaska Poem

The Hungry Dragonish Soul

The Raven Behind the Door

The Pelicans at White Horse Key

Rembrandt's Brown Ink

The Blinding of Samson

IV

Intuitions and Ideas

For MICHAEL VENTURA

A NOTE ABOUT THESE POEMS

I was surprised the other day as I read *The Light Around the Body*, a book of my own poems published in 1966, how little had changed since that time. We are still in blindfold, still being led by the wise of this world. I've taken a few poems from that old Sixties book and joined them with new ones for this collection. We are still causing endless suffering with our well-known nonchalance.

I.

When we think of it with this knowledge, we see that we have been locked up, and led blindfold, and it is the wise of this world who have shut and locked us up in their art and their rationality, so that we have had to see with their eyes.

— Jacob Boehme

What a distressing contrast there is between the radiant intelligence of the child, and the feeble mentality of the average adult.

— Sigmund Freud

CALL AND ANSWER

August 2002

Tell me why it is we don't lift our voices these days

And cry over what is happening. Have you noticed

The plans are made for Iraq and the ice cap is melting?

I say to myself: "Go on, cry. What's the sense

Of being an adult and having no voice? Cry out!

See who will answer! This is *Call and Answer!*"

We will have to call especially loud to reach

Our angels, who are hard of hearing; they are hiding

In the jugs of silence filled during our wars.

Have we agreed to so many wars that we can't

Escape from silence? If we don't lift our voices, we allow

Others (who are ourselves) to rob the house.

How come we've listened to the great criers—Neruda,

Akhmatova, Thoreau, Frederick Douglass—and now

We're silent as sparrows in the little bushes?

Some masters say our life lasts only seven days.

Where are we in the week? Is it Thursday yet?

Hurry, cry now! Soon Sunday night will come.

ADVICE FROM THE GEESE

Hurry! The world is not going to get better!

Do what you want to do now. The prologue is over.

Soon actors will come on stage carrying the coffin.

I don't want to frighten you, but not a stitch can be taken

On your quilt unless you study. The geese will tell you—

A lot of crying goes on before dawn comes.

Do you have a friend who has studied prisons?

Does a friend say: "I love the twelve houses"?

The word "houses" suggests prison all by itself.

So much suffering goes on among prisoners.

There is so much grief in the cells. So many bolts

Of lightning keep coming down from the unborn.

Please don't expect that the next President

Will be better than this one. Four o'clock

In the morning is the time to read Basilides.

Every seed spends many nights in the earth.

Give up the idea that the world will get better by itself.

You will not be forgiven if you refuse to study.

LET SYMPATHY PASS

1.

People vote for what will harm them; everywhere

Borks and thieves, bushes hung with union men.

Things are not well with us. Some deep-

Reaching covetousness rules the countryside.

The greedy one begins to eat Alaska,

The Caribbean Islands, the rainforests, the Tigris.

What did Whitman say a hundred years ago?

"Let sympathy pass, a stranger, to other shores!"

2.

When was it we wanted the holy mountains,

The Black Hills, what did we want them for?

Tamburlaine inhabits the autumnal woods;

Lame in one leg, half-mad, the old man

Inhabits the chambers of inaccessible oaks.

Didn't our race make a deal with the old man

So that the boy in the upper room would live?

Now boars rush in and out of the dusky surf.

3.

The two Bushes come. They say clearly they will

Make the rich richer, starve the homeless,

Tear down the schools, short-change the children,

And they are elected. Millions go to vote,

Vote to lose their houses, their pensions,

Lower their wages, bring themselves to dust.

All for the sake of whom? Oh you know —

That Secret Being, the old rapacious soul.

THE STEW OF DISCONTENTS

1.

Northern lights illumine the storm-troll's house.

There men murdered by God promenade.

The buffalo woman plays her bony flute calling

The lonely father trampled by the buffalo god.

The foreskins of angels shelter the naked cradle.

The stew of discontents feed the loose souls.

And the owl husbands the moors, harries the mouse,

Beforehand, behindhand, with his handsome eyes.

2.

The White House Administrator sits up late at night

Cutting his nails, and the backs of black whales, the tip

Of the mink's tail, the tongue that appears between lips,

All of these testify to a soul that eats and is eaten.

Pushed on by the inner pressure of teeth,

Some force, animal-born, is slippery, edgy,

Impatient, greedy to pray for new heavens,

Unforgiving, resentful, like a fire in dry wood.

3.

What will you say of our recent adventure?

Some element, Dresdenized, coated with Somme

Mud and flesh, entered, and all prayer was vain.

The Anglo-Saxon poets hear the whistle of the wild

Gander as it glides to the madman's hand.

Spent uranium floats into children's lungs.

All of the sake of whom? For him or her

Or it, the greedy one, the rapacious soul.

II.

For according to the outward man, we are in this world, and according to the inward man, we are in the inward world. . . . Since then we are generated out of both worlds, we speak in two languages, and we must be understood also by two languages.

—Jacob Boehme

THE EXECUTIVE'S DEATH

Merchants have multiplied more than the stars of heaven.

Half the population are like the long grasshoppers

That sleep in the bushes in the cool of the day:

The sound of their wings is heard at noon, muffled, near the
earth.

The crane handler dies, the taxi driver dies, slumped over

In his taxi. Meanwhile, high in the air, an executive

Walks on the cool floor, and suddenly falls.

He dreams he is lost in a snowstorm in a mountain,

On which he crashed, carried at night by great machines.

As he lies on the wintery slope, cut off and dying,

A pine stump talks to him of Goethe and Jesus.

Commuters arrive in Hartford at dusk like moles

Or hares flying from a fire behind them,

And the dusk in Hartford is full of their sighs;

Their trains come through the air like a dark music,

Like the sound of horns, the sound of thousands of small wings.

WATCHING TELEVISION

Sounds are heard too high for ears,

From the body cells there is an answering bay;

Soon the inner streets fill with a chorus of barks.

We see the landing craft coming in,

The black car sliding to a stop,

The Puritan killer loosening his guns.

Wild dogs tear off noses and eyes

And run off with them down the street—

The body tears off its own arms and throws them into the air.

The detective draws fifty-five million people into his revolver,

Who sleep restlessly as in an air raid in London;

Their backs become curved in the sloping dark.

The filaments of the soul slowly separate.

The spirit breaks, a puff of dust floats up,

Like a house on the Great Plains that suddenly explodes.

COME WITH ME

Come with me into those things that have felt this despair for so
 long—

Those removed Chevrolet wheels that howl with a terrible
 loneliness,

Lying on their backs in the cindery dirt, like men drunk and
 naked,

Staggering off down a hill at night to drown at last in a pond.

Those shredded inner tubes abandoned on the shoulders of
 thruways,

Black and collapsed bodies, that tried and burst, and were left
 behind.

And those curly steel shavings, scattered about on garage
 benches,

Sometimes still warm, gritty when we hold them,

Who have given up, and blame everything on the government;

And those roads in South Dakota that feel around in the dark-
 ness. . . .

THOSE BEING EATEN

The cry of those being eaten by America,

Others pale and soft being stored for later eating.

What of Jefferson

Who saw hope in new oats?

The wild houses go on

With long hair growing from between their toes.

The feet at night get up

And run down the long white roads by themselves.

Dams reverse themselves and want to go stand alone in the
    desert.

Ministers dive headfirst into the earth:

And the pale flesh

Spreads guiltily into new literatures.

That is why these poems are so sad:

The long dead running over the fields,

The mass sinking down,

The light in children's faces fading at six or seven.

The world will soon break up into small colonies of the saved.

A GLIMPSE OF AMERICAN HISTORY

If we go back, if we walk into the old darkness, we will find

Washington brooding under the long bridges,

The dead still ablaze in the anguish of the egg,

Screams reverberating in the compression chambers of shells,

Soldiers that disappear into the tunnels inside the flashlight,

Sioux bodies falling, and soap buried alive.

Sugarbeets that give blood migrate to the stars,

Drunken ward-heelers crawl in the icy gutters.

Our history is the story of something that failed:

A greedy fire is burning on our fingertips,

Fingers that turn over pages of deeds, fingers on fire,

Fingers that would light the sky if lifted at night.

SLEET STORM ON
THE MERRITT PARKWAY

I look out at the white sleet covering the still streets

As we drive through Scarsdale—

The sleet began falling as we left Connecticut,

And the winter leaves swirled in the wet air after cars

Like hands suddenly turned over in a conversation.

Now the frost has nearly buried the short grass of March.

Seeing the sheets of sleet untouched on the wide streets,

I think of the many comfortable homes stretching for miles,

Two and three stories, solid, with polished floors,

With white curtains in the upstairs bedrooms,

And small perfume flagons of black glass on the window sills,

And warm bathrooms with guest towels, and electric lights—

What a magnificent place for a child to grow up!

And yet the children end in the river of price-fixing,

Or in the snowy field of the insane asylum.

The sleet falls—so many cars moving toward New York—

Last night we argued about the Marines invading Guatemala in
    1947,

The United Fruit Company had one water spigor for 200
    families,

And the ideals of America, our freedom to criticize,

The slave systems of Rome and Greece, and no one agreed.

III.

O dear children, look in what a dungeon we are lying, in what lodging we are, for we have been captured by the spirit of the outward world; it is our life, for it nourishes and brings us up, it rules in our marrow and bones, in our flesh and blood, it has made our flesh earthly, and now death has us.

—Jacob Boehme

THE ALASKA POEM

There is so much forgotten rock in the world,

And so much blue, glacial ice crowding down to die,

So many overhangs on which petroglyphs are never found,

And so many ships that rise up and slip down with no iceberg
near.

There are stories long told that have never been understood,

And so many metaphors that Valentinus muttered to the frogs,

And so much wainscoting that widows have painted over,

And so many marriage stories that no one has understood.

We see houses in our dreams that need to be repaired,

We see horses that no one has fed for three weeks.

There are so many shoulders we should have touched with our
fingers,

And so many days when we forget we have a mother.

We drank down so many angers at our father's breast.

There are so many cries no one makes during the wedding
service.

There are so many poets whose poems no one reads.

There are so many pale bottles the demons set out for milk.

Some rivers go into a mountain and never come out again.

Boys ride rafts into a dark tunnel, and are gone.

Sometimes a mysterious man walks toward us—we hear him—

For days, for years, for sixty years, and never arrives.

THE HUNGRY DRAGONISH SOUL

1.

There are so many things at the edges,

The waning gibbous moon close to Jupiter in the dark,

Horses play in the darkening field.

What sort of god would make a world like this?

The father chopped off his daughter's fingers

As she climbed into his boat; all this chopping

Is done again and again in just this way.

All for the sake of whom? Best not to say.

2.

The guinea fowl cries so desolately; the gull

Calls from the mounds of refuse. The beaten

Woman howls; the calf is still half inside

The mother's womb. The deer is nearly down,

Paws pounce on the drop of blood. The young girl,

Whose father has left her bedroom — his shoulders slumped —

Sits cowed and empty on the side of her bed.

All is silent; no sounds come from the child.

3.

The wily bitter old man builds his manor house

Inside the stony chambers of inaccessible oaks.

The sunset gleams on his helmeted head.

The Baba Yaga cries out, "Did you come

Of your own free will or did someone send you?"

The hungry, dragonish soul, wakened from its

Long slumber, moves toward our wife and children.

The stew of discontents feeds the loose souls.

THE RAVEN BEHIND THE DOOR

1.

Living in Corsica, the one-eyed horseman knows

Who is behind the Door. For centuries he is there..

The men are mourning behind that door.

What is this fear? So many men hear

The sound of someone lapping stormy milk.

Is it a beast, or a woman, or a god,

A frightening thinker, or a snake with wings?

Someone who wants; the old desirous one.

2.

The man sits chewing the flint in his hard hands

While his wife moves among alien clouds.

Oh what has he given, to whom has he given it?

The rapacious soul says: Deepen your sleep..

Portia can grieve in her sorrowing house.

Let's force both mother and father to work.

Let's have the children come back to a cold house.

Saturn chews his son's arm down to the elbow joint.

3.

This poem will never be clear. You and I

Will never understand the insatiable soul.

Those who know their greedy soul know their lord.

Some power hides carefully behind our fathers,

Carefully behind our mothers, behind the poor's door.

Behind that door, a raven suffers from thirst;

Behind that, the god who refuses the raven water.

Behind that, the one who rules the sun and the moon.

THE PELICANS AT
WHITE HORSE KEY

Occasionally spreading their wings to the sun, pelicans

Dive for fish from dawn to dusk. The Lord of This World

Is a painter working at night in a dark room.

Earth is the place where we've agreed to throw

Away the gifts that Adam's grandfather gave us

During the dark time before eternity was born.

The lover's body belongs to ruined earth.

The scattered stars belong to the Milky Way.

The potato field belongs to early night.

The Monitor Lizard is a child of the Mother,

And a favorite child. The Monitor holds a snake

Immobile for an hour and then eats.

We know it's good not to have sharp opinions;

But would you still think so much of Noah

If he had thrown away his bag of nails?

Four times this month I have dreamt I am

A murderer; and I am. These lines are paper boats

Set out to float on the sea of repentance.

REMBRANDT'S BROWN INK

The sorrow of an old horse standing in the rain

Goes on and on. The plane that crashes in the desert

Holds shadows under its wings for thirty years.

Each time Rembrandt touches his pen to the page,

So many barns and fences fly up. Perhaps that's

Because earth has pulled so many nights down.

When we hear a Drupad singer with his low voice

Patiently waiting for the next breath, we know

The universe can easily get along without us.

So much suffering has been stored in the amygdala

That we know it won't be long before we put

Our heads down on the chopping block again.

The muscles of our thighs still remember those nights

When we crouched on the plains in the smoky

Dark keeping birds and small mammals in the cold.

How is it possible that so many nights of suffering

Could be summed up by a sketch in brown ink

Of Christ sitting at the table with Judas near?

THE BLINDING OF SAMSON

Don't you see them? They are coming to blind Samson!

But some of us don't want the day to end!

If Samson goes blind, what will happen to the sea?

Isn't it bad enough that the sun goes down

Each night, while children throw shoes at the moon?

I remember my mother's grief at sunset.

Now I remember my father. I remember

Every father when he is wrestling with his son.

Oh Lord of the Four Quarters—he is destined to lose!

You gypsy singers, make some raw cries!

Call in the crows to fly over the plowed fields.

I want the beating palms to cry out for Samson.

I want rough voices and shouting women

To cry out against the blinding of Samson.

I will always cry—take away those knives!

Isn't it enough that the Evening Star sets every night

And lovemaking ends at dawn? Please, God, help

The human beings, for men are coming to blind Samson.

IV.

TO THE STATES

To the States or any one of them, or any city of the States, Resist
  much, obey little,

Once unquestioning obedience, once fully enslaved,

Once fully enslaved, no nation, state, city of this earth, ever after-
  ward resumes its liberty.

—Walt Whitman

INTUITIONS AND IDEAS

People are amazed now when they read about the Lincoln-Douglas debates. The two of them would debate for six hours in the afternoon to large crowds, then take a break and come back for two or three hours more at night. Watching these men speak for hours, the listeners could see if the speakers' words fit the speakers' bodies. Is the language coming out of the face we see in front of us? Is that a genuine Lincoln and a genuine Douglas? But in the many plays we see on television each day, the speakers are always pretending to be someone else. So our citizens at a debate watch to see if the politicians are performing well in pretending to be someone else. Most voters have lost the ability to decide if a speaker's words do fit his or her body. That's why Bush—with the help of the Supreme Court—won the election. No one knows what to do about it.

*   *   *

More and more I've learned to respect the power of the phrase, "the greedy soul." We all understand what is hinted at with that phrase. It is the purpose of the United Nations to check the greedy soul in nations. It is the purpose of police to check the greedy soul in people. We know our soul has enormous abilities in worship and intuition coming to us from a very ancient past. But the greedy part of the soul—what the Muslims call "the nafs"—also receives its energy from a very ancient past. The nafs is the covetous, desirous, shameless energy that steals food from neighboring tribes, wants what it wants, and is willing to destroy anyone who receives more good things than itself. In a writer, it wants praise. I wrote three lines about it:

I live very close to my greedy soul.
When I see a book published two thousand years ago,
I check to see if my name is mentioned.

If the covetous soul feels that its national "sphere of influence" is being threatened by another country, it will kill recklessly and brutally, impoverish millions, order thousands of young men in its own country to be killed, only to find out thirty years later that the whole thing was a mistake. In politics, The Fog of War could also be called The Fog of the Greedy Soul.

*   *   *

England had an educated civil service that administered its empire. But the United States is more and more out of step with other Western nations, both in the intelligence of its leaders and the ability of its civil servants. We are shamefully behind France, Germany, Norway and Sweden, and far behind ourselves at the time of the Second World War.

*   *   *

You'll notice that we don't count civil Iraqi casualties in this war. We only count the American bodies. In Vietnam we did keep track of Vietnamese casualties. *The New York Times* reported on March 17, 2004, "Military officials say they do not have precise figures or even estimates of the number of non-combatant Iraqi's killed or wounded by American-led forces in Iraq. 'We don't keep a list,' said a Pentagon spokeswoman, Lt. Cmdr. Jane Campbell. 'It's just not policy'."

*   *   *

The invasion of Iraq is the biggest mistake any American Administration has ever made. The most dangerous and greatest confrontation is between twentieth-century capitalist fundamentalism and eleventh-century Muslim fundamentalism. There is much to admire in Muslim culture—immense delicacy and passion—but we're also looking at a society without any division between church and state, made monolithic by the mullahs in the eleventh century.

To increase the antagonism between the two systems is the worst choice possible for a Western country, and that is exactly what George Bush did. Bush Sr. was intelligent enough to pull back and not go towards Baghdad. To tear apart the beehive without any bee hats is a crazy act.

*   *   *

Many observers have noticed that even though the United States and Canada have many resemblances, we have so many more murders per thousand people than Canada does. Why is that? Perhaps it's because we kept slaves and later fought a vicious civil war to free or keep them. We know from Vietnam that the violence men witness or perform remains trapped in their bodies. That suffering Martín Prechtel has called "unmetabolized grief". To metabolize such grief would mean bringing the body slowly and gradually to absorb the grief into its own system, as it might some sort of poison. But the veterans of the Civil War received no such help. Once the Civil War was over, soldiers on both sides simply took off their uniforms. Some went west and became the Indian fighters. We have the stupidity typical of a country that doesn't realize what the killing of war can do to a human being. When the violent grief is unmetabolized, it demands to be repeated. One could say that we now have a compulsion to repeat the killing. Our Westerns have made that clear for decades.

Bush and Wolfowitz and Cheney are merely the highest placed men involved in the repetition compulsion. The need goes on below the level of rational thought. But it's wrong to give in to such men. We have veered off our own path, which after the Vietnam War has been for a while the path of repentance. In our mad way, we are spending millions to bomb and rebuild Iraq at the expense of our own health system, of education on all levels, and of the support of culture and science. Only the greedy soul could set aside five hundred million for a useless war in the same year that Oregon takes nineteen days off their school calendar.

The careful long-range planning that Eisenhower and others performed during and after the Second World War now seems beyond our power. We are not capable of empire, and we should admit that. The war is a hundred thousand men wandering about in the fog of the greedy soul.

TO THE STATES

To identify the 16th, 17th, or 18th Presidentiad

Why reclining, interrogating? why myself and all drowsing?

What deepening twilight - scum floating atop of the waters,

Who are they as bats and night-dogs askant in the capitol?

What a filthy Presidentiad! (O South, your torrid suns! O
    North, your arctic freezings!

Are those really Congressmen? are those the great Judges? is
    that the President?

Then I will sleep awhile yet, for I see that these States sleep, for
    reasons;

(With gathering murk, with muttering thunder and lambent
    shoots we all duly awake,

South, North, East, West, inland and seaboard, we will surely
    awake).

— Walt Whitman

ACKNOWLEDGEMENTS

We are grateful to HarperCollins for permission to publish several poems from *The Light Around the Body* ("Sleet Storm on the Merritt Parkway," "Those Being Eaten," "Come With Me," "Watching Television," and "The Executive's Death"), and one poem from *Meditations on the Insatiable Soul* ("The Alaska Poem").

"Call and Answer" originally appeared in *The Nation*; "Pelicans at White Horse Key" was published in *The Bitter Oleander*.